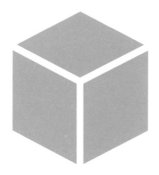

DEL REY
NEW YORK

Copyright © 2019 by Mojang AB and Mojang Synergies AB. MINECRAFT is a trademark or registered trademark of Mojang Synergies AB.

Published in the United States by Del Rey, an imprint of Random House, a division of Penguin Random House LLC, New York.

DEL REY and the HOUSE colophon are registered trademarks of Penguin Random House LLC.

Published in paperback in the United Kingdom by Egmont UK Limited.

ISBN 978-1-101-96638-9
Ebook ISBN 978-1-101-96639-6

Printed in China on acid-free paper by C & C Offset

Written by Stephanie Milton

Illustrations by Ryan Marsh

randomhousebooks.com

2 4 6 8 9 7 5 3

Design by Joe Bolder

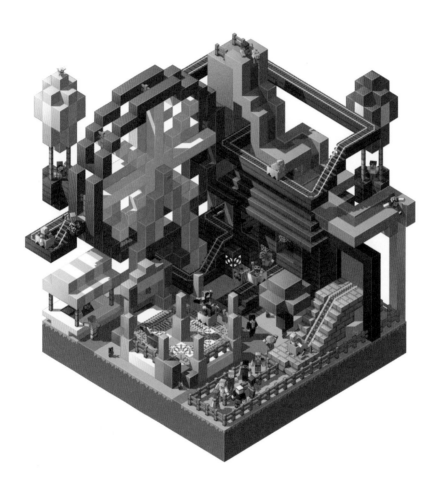

MOJANG

MINECRAFT™

LET'S BUILD!

THEME PARK
ADVENTURE

CONTENTS

HI FROM SPARKS

Welcome to *Theme Park Adventure*! My name is Sparks – I'm a redstone engineer and I just love building! I guess you do, too, which is why you've picked up this book. I also love theme parks and having fun, so this book is a combination of all my favorite things, really.

I love my friends, too, and they helped me test out all my ideas when I was building my theme park. I've been known to get a little carried away inventing things... Anyway, let me introduce you: there's Bear, the survival expert, who's stealthy like a ninja; Scout, who's a combat expert and isn't afraid of anything; and Monty, who loves studying nature and is extremely fond of food.

We've got quite an adventure in store for you! Together we're going to build the most epic theme park you've ever seen. It'll be full of all sorts of exciting rides, and your friends are going to be super impressed with your building skills!

Before we begin, I have a couple of pro tips for you:

1. You're going to want to build everything in Creative mode. Just trust me.

2. You'll need to track down a woodland mansion in a dark forest biome and start building your theme park from there – when you get to the page about the Haunted Mansion Ride, you'll see why! If you're struggling to find a woodland mansion, find an NPC village and trade with a friendly cartographer until they offer you an explorer map. That'll lead you straight to your nearest woodland mansion.

Let's get started! **Yaaaaay!**

BOUNCY CASTLE

Let's start with something nice and simple that everyone can enjoy – even people who are afraid of roller coasters! Slime blocks are super bouncy, and they're perfect for making a bouncy castle. I just love bouncing, don't you?

HI, I'M SPARKS!

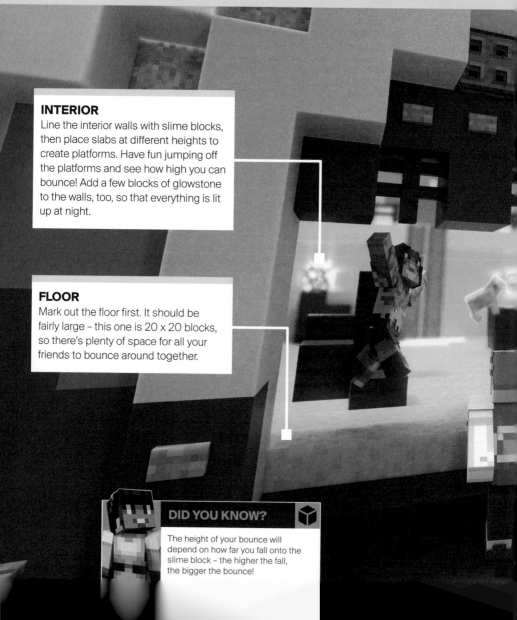

INTERIOR

Line the interior walls with slime blocks, then place slabs at different heights to create platforms. Have fun jumping off the platforms and see how high you can bounce! Add a few blocks of glowstone to the walls, too, so that everything is lit up at night.

FLOOR

Mark out the floor first. It should be fairly large – this one is 20 x 20 blocks, so there's plenty of space for all your friends to bounce around together.

DID YOU KNOW?

The height of your bounce will depend on how far you fall onto the slime block – the higher the fall, the bigger the bounce!

WHEEEE!

EXTERIOR
Build the exterior of your castle from colorful concrete blocks, in the shape of a small castle. Create four walls with a small turret in each corner and crenels (arrow holes) along the top. You don't need a roof for your castle.

TIP !

Theme park rides are often built close together and sometimes overlap. As you add each new ride or feature, think about how you can build it around your existing rides so everything is within walking distance.

BOUNCY DESIGNS

Fancy building something less traditional? There are all sorts of bouncy castle designs you could try. Here are a couple of my favorites!

CREEPER HEAD BOUNCY HOUSE

To be honest, I'm not super fond of creepers, but there's no denying this creeper head bouncy house looks amazing! I built it from concrete blocks, and you enter through the creeper's open mouth. Are you brave enough to go inside, though? Eek!

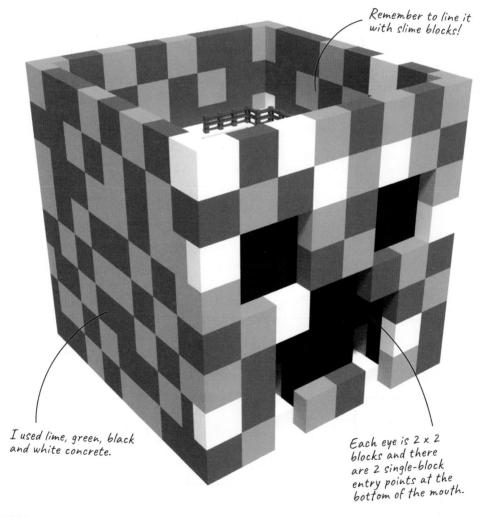

Remember to line it with slime blocks!

I used lime, green, black and white concrete.

Each eye is 2 x 2 blocks and there are 2 single-block entry points at the bottom of the mouth.

BOUNCY MANSION

Why stop at just one room when you can bounce your way around an entire mansion? To make it even more fun, you can create extra bouncy sections using a clever bit of redstone called a clock circuit, attached to 1 sticky piston and 12 slime blocks. Use these as platforms to bounce over walls from one room to another.

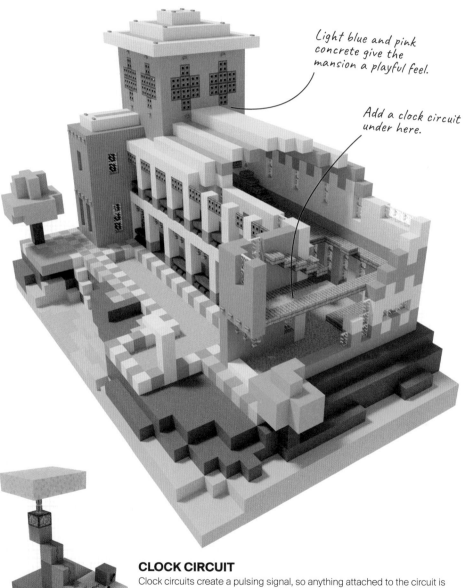

Light blue and pink concrete give the mansion a playful feel.

Add a clock circuit under here.

CLOCK CIRCUIT

Clock circuits create a pulsing signal, so anything attached to the circuit is repeatedly activated. In this case, the sticky piston is repeatedly powered, which means the slime block is pushed up and you'll bounce even higher.

CLASSIC CAROUSEL

No theme park would be complete without a classic carousel! They're easy to build and you can have loads of fun decorating them. Let me walk you through the features of this classic design.

ROOF
Carousels usually have conical (cone-shaped) roofs. You can use stair blocks to create this effect and taper them up toward the center of the roof.

SUPPORTS
Run 4 lines of End rods or fence posts from the roof down to the base of your carousel. These look like the roof supports you often see on a real-life classic carousel.

BASE
Try building out 6 blocks in each direction from your central pillar to create a good-sized base for your ride. I used wood planks to give my carousel a vintage feel.

HORSES
Lead saddled horses toward the mine carts and give them a little push until they're inside the carts. Now grab your friends, jump on and enjoy the ride!

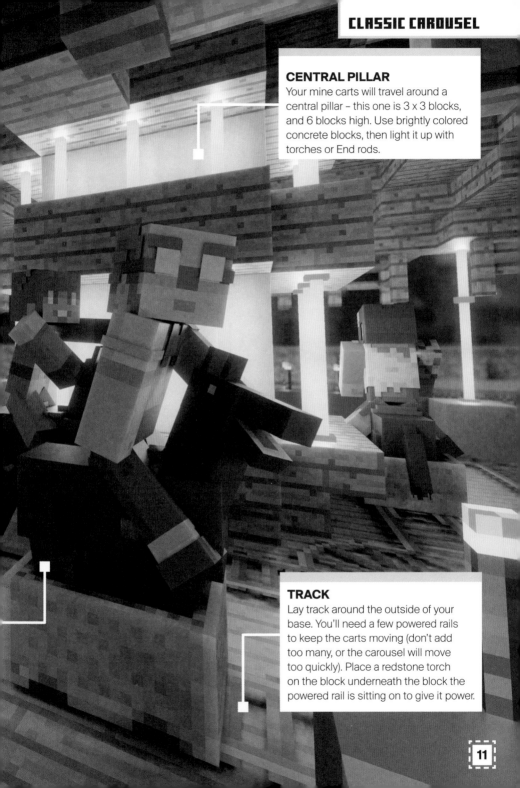

CENTRAL PILLAR

Your mine carts will travel around a central pillar – this one is 3 x 3 blocks, and 6 blocks high. Use brightly colored concrete blocks, then light it up with torches or End rods.

TRACK

Lay track around the outside of your base. You'll need a few powered rails to keep the carts moving (don't add too many, or the carousel will move too quickly). Place a redstone torch on the block underneath the block the powered rail is sitting on to give it power.

NOT-SO-CLASSIC CAROUSELS

I've had so much fun experimenting with different carousel designs – horses aren't the only rideable animal in Minecraft, after all! Here are some awesome theme ideas that you might want to try out if you're looking for something less traditional.

PINK PIG CAROUSEL

Monty loves pigs, so I built him a pink pig carousel. The structure is made from pink concrete, and I placed saddled pigs in the mine carts. Pigs love carrots, so I put some in item frames to decorate the central pillar. Unfortunately, you can't turn pink concrete into stair blocks, so I gave this one a flat roof instead.

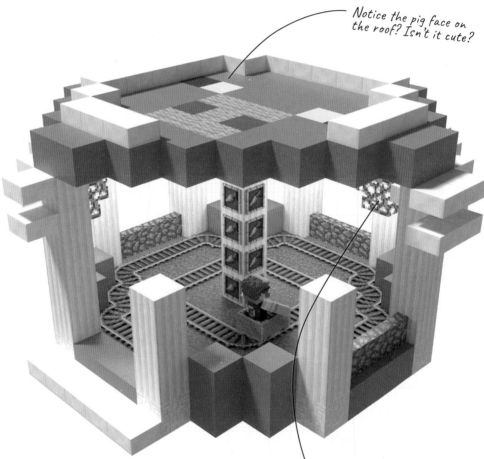

Notice the pig face on the roof? Isn't it cute?

I used glowstone blocks to light up the carousel.

LLAMA CAROUSEL

I think llamas might be the funniest animals in Minecraft! They can be found in savanna and mountain biomes, and can be ridden and equipped with chests and carpets. I thought they'd be perfect for this alternative carousel design.

The central pillar is built from wool to complement the llama's carpets.

Banners make a great addition to this design.

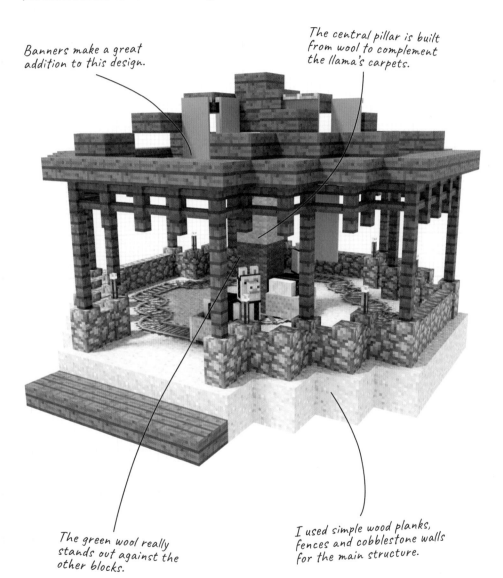

The green wool really stands out against the other blocks.

I used simple wood planks, fences and cobblestone walls for the main structure.

AROUND THE OVERWORLD

HI, I'M MONTY!

If, like Monty, you love to explore the natural world, this is the ride for you. Take a leisurely boat trip through a miniature version of a Minecraft world featuring all the major biomes. You'll be able to watch the Overworld's most dangerous mobs in their natural habitats in complete safety!

LAYOUT

Divide the river into zones – you can group your biomes however you like, but Monty told me to group them by temperature. The ride starts with the dry/warm biomes, moves on to the medium/lush biomes, then to the snowy/cold biomes. I divided the river into sections and started a new biome every 30 blocks along the banks.

LOCATION

Find a large area of flat land, ideally with an existing river running through it so that you don't have to build one. You'll need to build a structure around the ride when it's finished – you don't want daylight killing off any sun-sensitive hostile mobs!

IF YOU CAN GET PAST THE SPITTING, LLAMAS ARE QUITE FASCINATING.

DID YOU KNOW?

You won't find barrier blocks in your inventory. With your game open, type this command: /give @s barrier. A barrier block will appear in your hotbar, ready for you to use. So clever!

LIGHTING

Since your ride will be indoors, you'll need to light it up. Try to use light sources that might naturally be found in each biome – you could add lava pools in plains biomes and torches to any villages, for example. If no light source occurs naturally, use torches.

MOBS

You don't want mobs wandering off into other biomes. This is where barrier blocks come in handy – they're invisible solid blocks that you can use to build a wall around each biome.

BOATS

Your friends will collect a boat from a dispenser at the beginning of the ride. They'll be in charge of sailing themselves around the ride and will need to return their boats by placing them in a chest at the end.

OVERWORLD DETAILS

Let's take a look at some of the details you may want to include for each biome of your Around the Overworld Ride – it's important to get the terrain right, and to include some key, naturally generated structures and mobs.

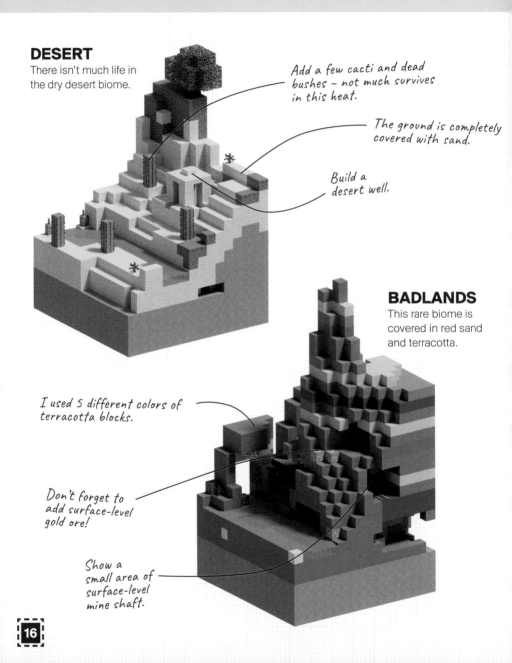

DESERT

There isn't much life in the dry desert biome.

Add a few cacti and dead bushes – not much survives in this heat.

The ground is completely covered with sand.

Build a desert well.

BADLANDS

This rare biome is covered in red sand and terracotta.

I used 5 different colors of terracotta blocks.

Don't forget to add surface-level gold ore!

Show a small area of surface-level mine shaft.

PLAINS

This grassy biome is one of the only places horses generate naturally.

Add a lava pool.

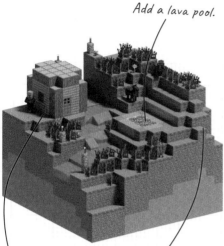

Build a small plains village and spawn some villagers.

Lay grass blocks as far as the eye can see!

SAVANNA

Savannas are flat and covered in dry grass.

You'll need lots of grass and some acacia trees.

Spawn a family of llamas – they love it here!

FOREST

There's no shortage of oak trees in the forest biome.

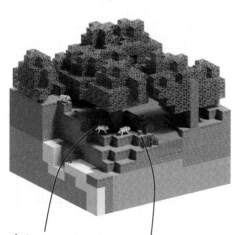

A forest isn't a forest without a pack of wild wolves!

Plant some pretty dandelions and poppies.

DARK FOREST

This is a gloomy biome due to the huge mushrooms and densely packed trees.

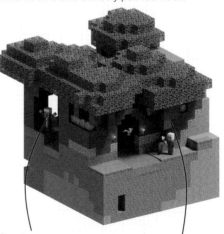

Don't forget the vindicator, evoker and vex inside the mansion.

Build a small section of woodland mansion.

SWAMP

There's lots of surface water in swamp biomes.

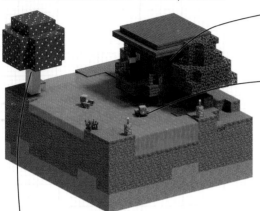

Build a witch hut
and spawn a witch.

Drowned mobs like
to hang out in damp
swamp biomes.

Add a few swamp trees
and huge mushrooms.

MUSHROOM FIELDS

This strange biome is covered in mycelium
and mushrooms.

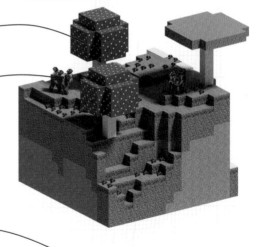

Apply bone meal to mushrooms
to create huge mushrooms.

Spawn a family of
gentle mooshrooms.

JUNGLE

Jungles are packed with life and are home
to some very tall trees.

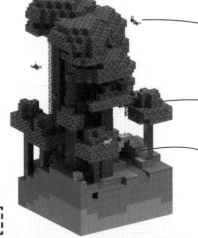

Spawn lots of parrots
and a few ocelots.

You'll need several jungle trees
with cocoa pods growing on
their trunks.

Build a small section of
jungle temple.

TAIGA

Taiga biomes are covered in spruce trees.

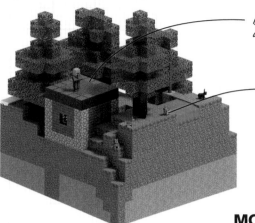

Build a small taiga village and spawn some villagers.

Spawn a few salt-and-pepper and black rabbits.

MOUNTAINS

This highland biome is mainly composed of stone.

Spawn a herd of llamas.

Show a cave just below ground level containing a single block of emerald ore.

Monster eggs can be found underground – they release silverfish when mined.

SNOWY TUNDRA

You'll find a lot of snow and ice here.

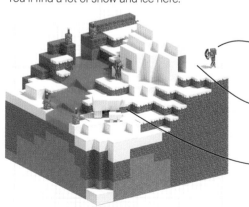

Spawn some strays.

Build an igloo from snow and ice.

Don't forget to add a polar bear family!

EPIC WATER SLIDE

There's nothing more refreshing than splashing around on a water slide on a sunny day. This slide has plenty of twists, turns and drops as it sends you on a journey down the side of this steep hill, then deposits you into the ocean for the final splashdown!

HI, I'M BEAR!

LOCATION
Find the biggest hill you can (mountain biomes are best), ideally facing an ocean. If you can't find a hill on the edge of the ocean, you can build a splash pool for the end instead.

DAREDEVIL DROPS
These drops send players plummeting over the edge of your slide and free falling for a few blocks before landing in another section of slide below. Turn the page for a tutorial.

TIP !
Water will flow 8 blocks along a flat surface before stopping. So, for any flat areas of your slide, you'll need to create a new water source block every 8 blocks, or lower the eighth block so the water continues to move.

MATERIALS

Bright concrete blocks are perfect! Use blue if you want the slide to blend in with the water, or red, yellow and orange if you want the slide to contrast with the water.

DARK SECTIONS

Some parts of the ride could travel inside the hill and through a few gloomy caves, or give some areas of your slide a roof so riders are plunged into darkness.

ROUTE

Build steps up the side of your hill to the start of the ride. Mark out a route for your slide – it will need to snake down the hillside with as many twists, turns and drops as possible. This slide is 3 blocks wide – you don't want it to be too narrow.

WHEEE! I LOVE A WATER SLIDE!

DAREDEVIL DROPS

Daredevil drops can be tricky to build, and it's really important that you get them right – otherwise your friends will shoot right over the slide and plummet to the ground below! Follow these steps and you can't go wrong.

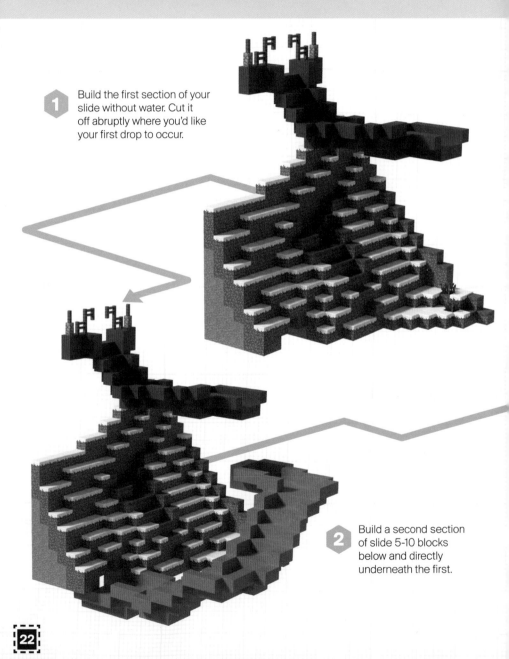

1 Build the first section of your slide without water. Cut it off abruptly where you'd like your first drop to occur.

2 Build a second section of slide 5-10 blocks below and directly underneath the first.

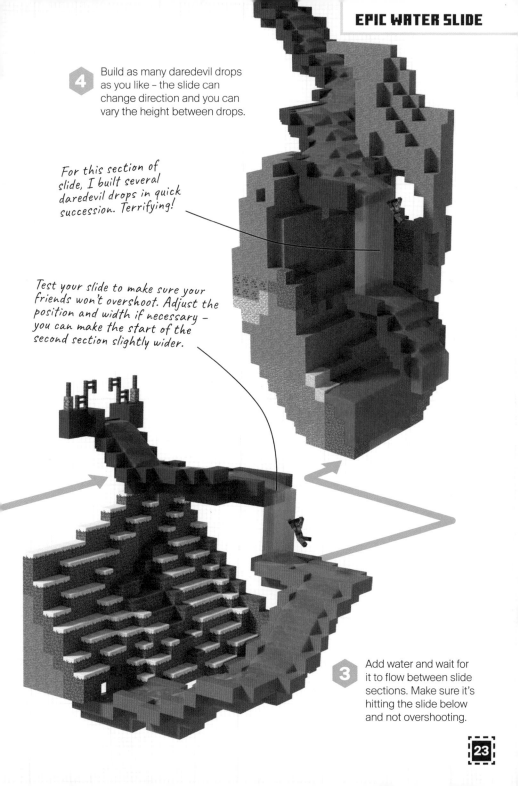

4 Build as many daredevil drops as you like – the slide can change direction and you can vary the height between drops.

For this section of slide, I built several daredevil drops in quick succession. Terrifying!

Test your slide to make sure your friends won't overshoot. Adjust the position and width if necessary – you can make the start of the second section slightly wider.

3 Add water and wait for it to flow between slide sections. Make sure it's hitting the slide below and not overshooting.

DARING DESIGNS

I had so much fun building my water slide that I decided to build several different versions around my park! Here are some daring designs for you to try out.

ICE SLIDE

If you're near a cold or snowy biome, or even if you're not, you can create an ice slide! Be warned – this one is faster than the others!

Find a cold or snowy biome for this one if you can.

Don't place torches or other light sources nearby – they'll melt the ice!

Water flows faster over ice.

BLACK HOLE

Build a black hole slide from black concrete and add a roof to the entire slide. Light up the inside using End rods or glowstone blocks.

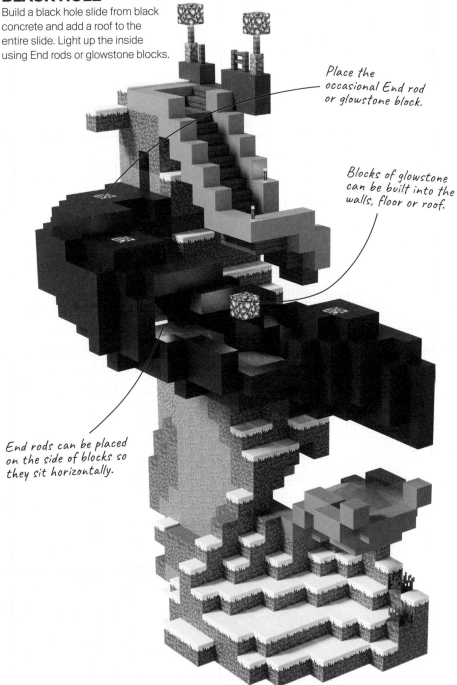

Place the occasional End rod or glowstone block.

Blocks of glowstone can be built into the walls, floor or roof.

End rods can be placed on the side of blocks so they sit horizontally.

JUNGLE RIVER RAPIDS

Wild, overgrown jungle biomes are the perfect backdrop for some frenzied, fast-paced river rapids. Full of twists and turns, as well as obstacles for you to steer around, this is no easy ride, but it's a lot of fun!

HI, I'M SCOUT!

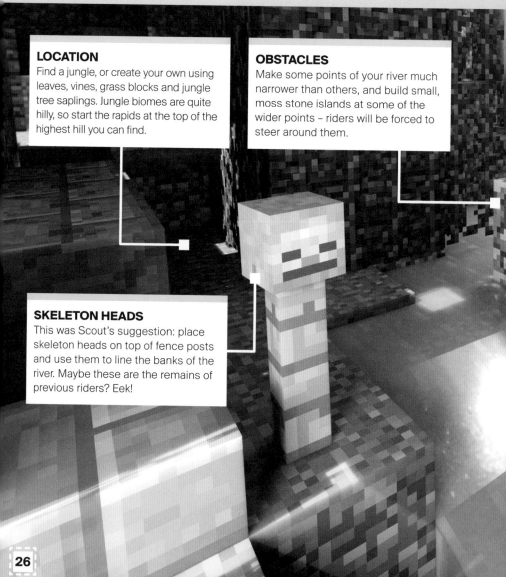

LOCATION
Find a jungle, or create your own using leaves, vines, grass blocks and jungle tree saplings. Jungle biomes are quite hilly, so start the rapids at the top of the highest hill you can find.

OBSTACLES
Make some points of your river much narrower than others, and build small, moss stone islands at some of the wider points – riders will be forced to steer around them.

SKELETON HEADS
This was Scout's suggestion: place skeleton heads on top of fence posts and use them to line the banks of the river. Maybe these are the remains of previous riders? Eek!

WATERFALL DROPS

Add a few waterfall drops to keep things interesting. You can also create waterfalls at the side of the river which flow into it and help to create chaotic water flow.

ANCIENT RUINS

Take your ride through some custom-made, ancient ruins. Build them out of moss stone, cobblestone and chiseled stone bricks and cover them in vines to get the aged effect. You could build the remains of walls and pillars on the banks of the river, construct arches that span the river or even take the river through the remains of a temple.

TO BEAT THE RIVER, WE MUST BECOME THE RIVER!

TWISTS AND TURNS

Carve out an exciting route for your rapids as they travel downhill, with as many twists and turns as you can fit in. Once you're happy with the route, add water.

BOATS

Place a dispenser at the start of the ride with a sign advising each person to take several boats. Trust me – some will break during the course of the rapids!

ANCIENT RUINS

Follow these step-by-step guides to create some very convincing ancient ruins for your rapids. They'll be so good, your friends will think they've discovered a lost world!

TEMPLE REMAINS

I built these temple remains from moss stone, chiseled stone bricks and vines. I wanted the remains to look different from the naturally occurring jungle temples, so I used a pyramid design.

Add trees and leaves to any gaps to make it feel overgrown.

I built the temple into the side of a hill.

Carve a route for the river right through the center.

Add a few drops to make it exciting.

ANCIENT PILLARS

Build pillars out of stone brick, but leave deliberate gaps to make them look like they're crumbling away.

Use slabs to build a wide top to match the base.

Build upward from the base using stone brick blocks.

Cover the pillar with vines.

Use slabs to build a wide base for your pillar.

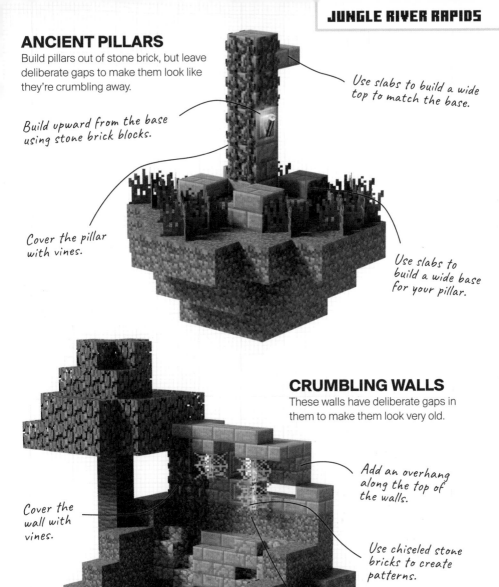

CRUMBLING WALLS

These walls have deliberate gaps in them to make them look very old.

Add an overhang along the top of the walls.

Cover the wall with vines.

Use chiseled stone bricks to create patterns.

Add a few cobwebs underneath the overhang.

STRANGE STATUES

Jungles are so mysterious! Who built the temples? Why are creepers afraid of ocelots? Will we ever know? These strange statues will add to the air of mystery – use them to line the banks of the river for your rapids.

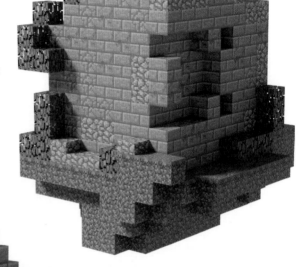

FALLEN CREEPER STATUE

This ancient creeper statue looks like it fell over many years ago – now it's crumbling away among the bushes at the side of the river. So sad!

OCELOT STATUE

Did you know that ancient civilizations used to worship cats? Ocelots scare creepers away, which explains why someone like me would want to build a statue to celebrate them. I hate creepers!

FACELESS PLAYER STATUES

I've always been curious about the mysterious jungle temples, so I built these faceless statues in honor of the ancient people who built them.

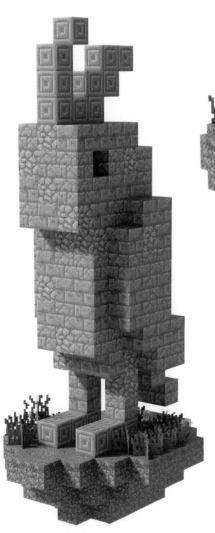

PARROT STATUE

You can't visit a jungle biome without seeing these delightfully colorful birds. Monty named this one Algernon.

BOWL WATER SLIDE

Ooh, goody! Another water slide! This one starts off as a regular water slide but deposits players into several large bowls with holes in the bottom. Gravity pulls them through the holes and into the next section of ride below. It's a bit like being sucked down several plug holes!

LOCATION

This is best built as a freestanding slide rather than against a cliff. You'll need quite a bit of space – I used an area of around 45 x 45 x 45 blocks.

BOWLS

This bowl slide has 3 bowls, each separated by sections of regular slide. The lowest bowl deposits riders into a splash pool at the end of the ride. Turn the page for a bowl tutorial.

TIP !

Build this slide right next to the first water slide, then design the surrounding area to look like a beach. See page 59 for beach ideas.

MATERIALS

I love all the colors of the rainbow! I used red, orange, yellow, lime, light blue, blue and purple concrete to build a stripy slide and rainbow bowls.

ROUTE

Choose a route for your slide that works in the space you have. This one is a giant spiral, which adds to the dizzying effect of being pulled into the center of the bowls.

THE BOWLS

Bowls might look tricky to make, but they're actually really easy when you know how! Let me talk you through the build process for my rainbow bowls so you can see how it's done.

1 Make a ring of blocks with a cross-shaped hole in the center. This will form the bottom of the bowl – the hole through which players are pulled into the next section of the slide.

Be sure to leave a cross-shaped, 5 x 5 block hole in the center.

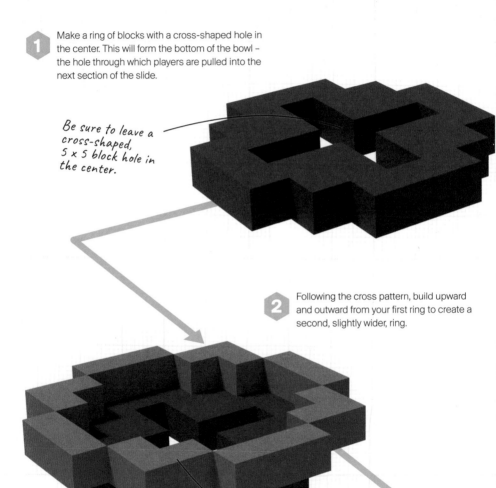

2 Following the cross pattern, build upward and outward from your first ring to create a second, slightly wider, ring.

I used a different color concrete block for each layer, to make my bowl look like a rainbow.

5 Build the next section of your slide directly under the hole in the bowl. Finally, add water, wait for it to fill the bowl, then give it a go!

4 Now join the bowl to a section of your water slide higher up, so that players will shoot down the slide and into the bowl.

Now the bowl is really starting to look like a rainbow!

3 Repeat step 2 until you've created a bowl of the desired depth – this one is 7 blocks high.

ALTERNATIVE THEMES

What's that? You had so much fun building your rainbow water slide that you want to build another? Me, too, which is why I came up with these alternative designs!

OCEAN MONUMENT

I discovered an ocean monument on my travels, and it inspired me to create this bowl slide. Don't you just love the color of prismarine? It's so pretty!

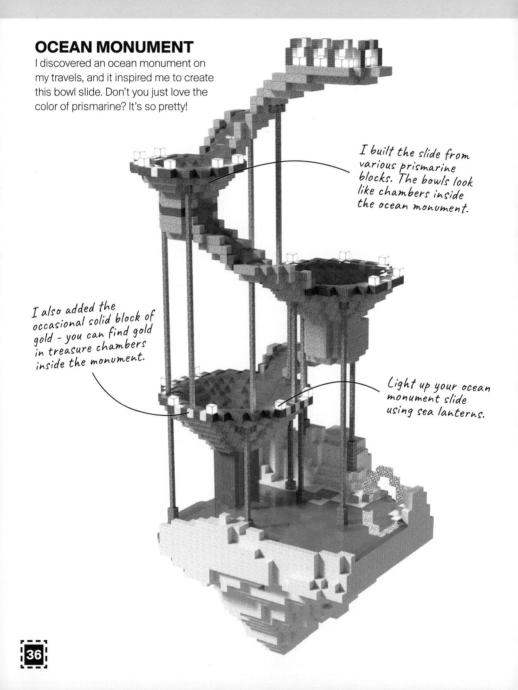

I built the slide from various prismarine blocks. The bowls look like chambers inside the ocean monument.

I also added the occasional solid block of gold - you can find gold in treasure chambers inside the monument.

Light up your ocean monument slide using sea lanterns.

THE VOID

Inspired by The Void, this bowl water slide is completely enclosed with only a few dim light sources. It's extra terrifying!

The Void sits right underneath the bedrock layer at the bottom of the world, so I built bedrock pillars to support it.

Use black concrete to construct this slide. You want it to be as dark as possible.

Use a few End rods to cast a dim light in the bowl sections.

HAUNTED MANSION RIDE

Eek! This woodland mansion was scary enough to begin with, but we're going to make it extra terrifying. Prepare for some spooky surprises as this thrilling ride takes you rattling around the house of horrors. Bear's going to love it!

MOB CELLS

Turn some of the rooms along each corridor into hostile mob cells – keeping mobs in sealed-off areas rather than wandering the corridors stops them from interfering with your ride. You can trap anything from zombies to ghasts inside them by blocking the entrances with iron bars. I don't mind admitting I had to get Bear and Scout to help me with this bit...

SPOOKY SOUNDTRACK

Place jukeboxes on each floor and play creepy music discs to create a fittingly frightening soundtrack – the discs that freak me out the most are 11, 13 and the disc called "ward." Remember to manually restart every jukebox at the end of each disc.

BE AT ONE WITH THE SHADOWS!

DID YOU KNOW?

Every woodland mansion has a slightly different layout. So, although your ride won't look exactly like this one, I'm sure it'll be just as awesome!

LIGHT

You don't want daylight streaming in and ruining the atmosphere, so block up the windows with soul sand (notice the creepy face in the texture?). Switch the regular torches for redstone torches – they'll create a dimmer glow.

CREEPY DETAILS

Scour your inventory for the creepiest items you can find. There are several skeleton paintings that would look super scary on the walls, and you can scatter all those horrible mob heads around the mansion. There's nothing more horrifying than a disembodied head...

NATURAL TOUCHES

Knock a few holes in the floor around the track to give the ride a rickety, precarious feel. Fill empty space with cobwebs and mushrooms to give the mansion an air of neglect.

EEEEEEEK!

TIP

Remember the tip I gave you on page 5? This ride is the reason you need to find a dark forest biome - it'd take a long time to build this mansion from scratch!

RIDE MECHANICS

Need some help to get the mine-cart ride right? This is totally my favorite part of creating this ride – loads of redstone to play with and no hostile mobs to worry about! Let's take a look at how to put the ride together and how the redstone mechanics work.

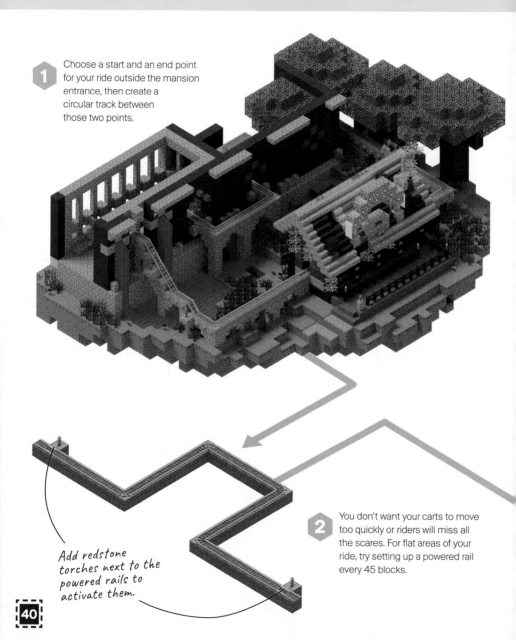

1 Choose a start and an end point for your ride outside the mansion entrance, then create a circular track between those two points.

Add redstone torches next to the powered rails to activate them.

2 You don't want your carts to move too quickly or riders will miss all the scares. For flat areas of your ride, try setting up a powered rail every 45 blocks.

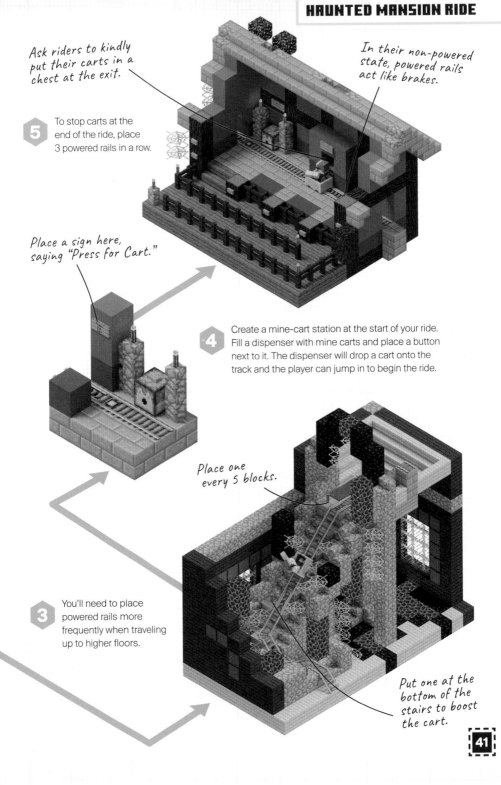

Ask riders to kindly put their carts in a chest at the exit.

In their non-powered state, powered rails act like brakes.

5 To stop carts at the end of the ride, place 3 powered rails in a row.

Place a sign here, saying "Press for Cart."

4 Create a mine-cart station at the start of your ride. Fill a dispenser with mine carts and place a button next to it. The dispenser will drop a cart onto the track and the player can jump in to begin the ride.

Place one every 5 blocks.

3 You'll need to place powered rails more frequently when traveling up to higher floors.

Put one at the bottom of the stairs to boost the cart.

ROOFTOP GRAVEYARD

Fancy an extra build challenge? Of course you do! Woodland mansions have a flat area of roof. With a little imagination, you can turn this into a spooky graveyard, then extend your ride so that it travels around it.

1 Replace the roof's wood planks with grass, then choose a route for your mine cart and lay the track.

2 There are several ways to build gravestones. You can place mob heads on a variety of blocks or anvils. You can also use step blocks.

3 You'll want to block out some of the sunlight from overhead. Build some spooky trees using wood, leaves and cobwebs, and extend the canopies over the graves.

KEEP CALM, NOTHING WE CAN'T HANDLE!

TIP

Use bone meal on grass blocks to make tall grass and flowers appear around your graves.

4 If you're feeling particularly creative, you could build a super creepy tomb or crypt. If the lighting is low enough and the design allows, you could trap some zombies in there for added scare-factor.

5 In front of each gravestone, you could place 2 dirt blocks to look like freshly dug earth, or you could use stone blocks.

I DON'T LIKE IT!

RUNAWAY MINE CART RIDE

I don't know about you, but I find abandoned mine shafts extremely creepy. All those dark tunnels and cave spiders make me shudder, but I promised Scout I'd build her a Runaway Mine Cart Ride. I hope you're ready for this!

LOCATION

Abandoned mine shafts are fairly common, so you should be able to find one a little way below the surface somewhere within your park. If you're near a badlands biome, there might even be one at surface level. If you can't track one down, find a cave system or ravine and build your own – you'll just need wood planks, fences, rails and torches.

DAREDEVIL DROPS

Remember the daredevil drops you made for your water slide? We're going to make some for this ride, too – abandoned mine shafts often have missing sections of track, so they're the perfect feature to include. Turn the page for a tutorial.

TRACK

Your mine carts should move quickly, especially in places where the track is precariously positioned above a long drop – as the name of this ride suggests, you want riders to feel like the mine cart has run away. Don't be afraid to include plenty of steep drops. You'll need to use lots of powered rails, especially in places where your ride travels upward.

CAVE SPIDER SPAWNER
Take the ride through a giant cluster of cobwebs and cave spider spawners. Gaa – I hate spiders! Are they on me? I feel like they're on me!

ENTRANCE
The ride starts and finishes at surface level – there's a sharp drop right at the beginning of the ride as the mine carts descend from the surface into the mine shaft.

I EAT CAVE SPIDERS FOR BREAKFAST!

TRACK ROUTE
Mark out a route around your abandoned mine shaft using wood planks. In some places, you can use the existing mine shaft tunnels; in others you can take your track along dangerous cliff faces and across steep drops. You want this ride to feel old and rickety – as if it could collapse at any moment.

TIP !
Remember everything you learned about powering rails with redstone from the Haunted Mansion Ride – you're going to need lots of powered rails for this ride, too!

45

DAREDEVIL DROPS

Accuracy is super important when it comes to making daredevil drops for your Runaway Mine Cart Ride. When they are done correctly, they look dangerous but are actually quite safe. Follow these steps to create the perfect scare.

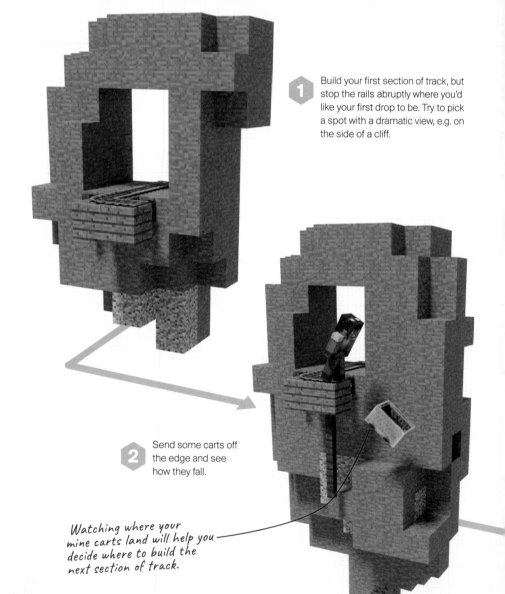

1 Build your first section of track, but stop the rails abruptly where you'd like your first drop to be. Try to pick a spot with a dramatic view, e.g. on the side of a cliff.

2 Send some carts off the edge and see how they fall.

Watching where your mine carts land will help you decide where to build the next section of track.

5 Create several more drops to give riders a nail-biting experience. Don't forget to test each drop as you create it to make sure it works!

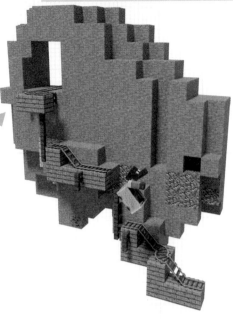

Send some more carts off the edge of the first section of track and make sure they hit the track below.

4

If your cart doesn't land on the next section of track, move the track and try again!

3 Build the next section of track a few blocks below the first, in the spot where you think your mine carts will land.

LOST TREASURE VAULT

Abandoned mine shafts are another great mystery – nobody really knows who built them. What we do know is that they were built so that valuable ores could be mined more easily, and this inspired me to create a lost treasure vault at the end of my ride. Here's how to make it!

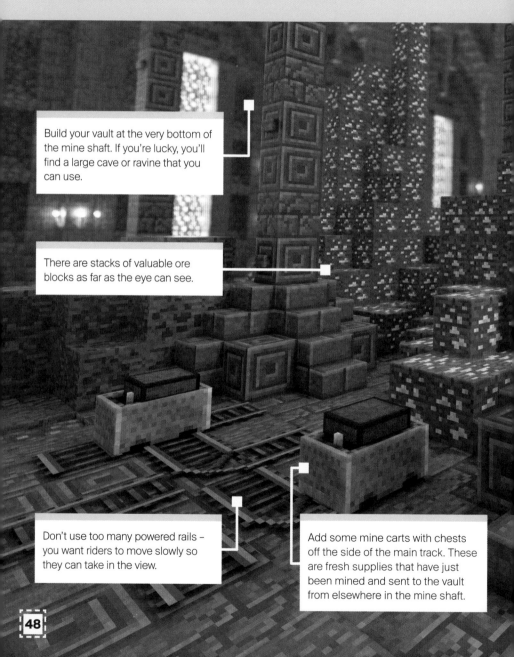

Build your vault at the very bottom of the mine shaft. If you're lucky, you'll find a large cave or ravine that you can use.

There are stacks of valuable ore blocks as far as the eye can see.

Don't use too many powered rails – you want riders to move slowly so they can take in the view.

Add some mine carts with chests off the side of the main track. These are fresh supplies that have just been mined and sent to the vault from elsewhere in the mine shaft.

Stack the blocks as high as you like and run your track right through the center of the vault.

There are also solid blocks of diamond, gold, iron and emerald stacked across the vault.

Don't forget to light it up with torches and lava!

Chests are dotted around in among the blocks – they must contain valuable treasures!

ALTERNATE DIMENSIONS RIDE

This scary Alternate Dimensions Ride is the ultimate thrill. Although it's created in the Overworld, you'll feel as if you've been plunged into the fiery depths of the Nether, before being whisked off to the terrifying End dimension. Let's take a look at the Nether section first.

NETHER TERRAIN
Build a giant obsidian frame at the start – riders will feel like they're traveling through a Nether portal. Create terrain using netherrack, magma blocks and lava.

TIP !

This ride is best enclosed in a simple building to keep it dark and atmospheric. Mark out a rectangular space for your ride, then try to keep the track within the corners of this structure. Construct the building once your ride is complete – this one's made from black concrete.

GHAST
Take your ride through a giant model of a ghast in attack mode – the track could enter through the mouth and exit through the back of its head.

END PORTAL
Time to change dimensions! At the end of your Nether section, take your track down a steep drop and through a giant ring of End portal blocks.

I LAUGH IN THE FACE OF GHASTS! AHAHAHA!

TRACK ROUTE
Take your track through several lavafalls and build a small area of Nether fortress for the track to travel through.

51

NETHER FEATURES

Let's take a closer look at how to construct some of the trickier Nether features for your Alternate Dimensions Ride. The more detail you include, the scarier your ride will feel!

GHAST HEAD

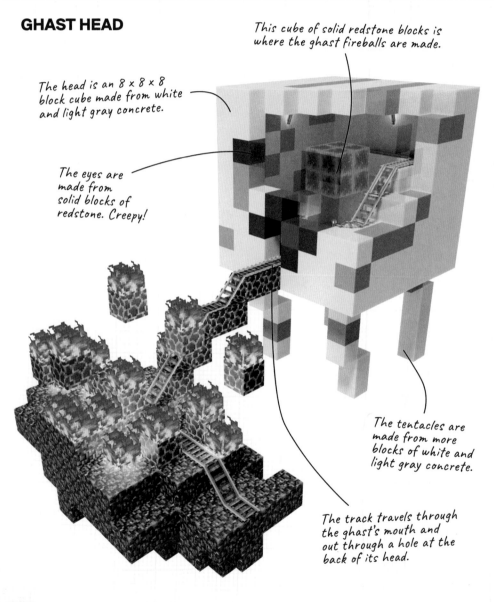

This cube of solid redstone blocks is where the ghast fireballs are made.

The head is an 8 x 8 x 8 block cube made from white and light gray concrete.

The eyes are made from solid blocks of redstone. Creepy!

The tentacles are made from more blocks of white and light gray concrete.

The track travels through the ghast's mouth and out through a hole at the back of its head.

NETHER FORTRESS

Make the blaze spawner platform larger than the real thing so there's plenty of space.

Build a pillar, a corridor and a blaze spawner platform.

Nether fortresses are built from Nether brick.

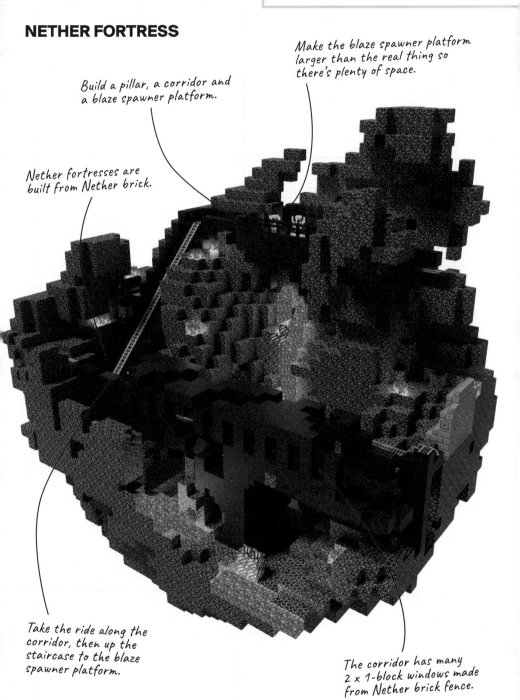

Take the ride along the corridor, then up the staircase to the blaze spawner platform.

The corridor has many 2 x 1-block windows made from Nether brick fence.

RIDE TO THE END

Phew – it's out of the frying pan and into the fire! Let me talk you through how I created the End section of this terrifying ride. This is a miniature version of the entire End dimension, with all the features mixed up over several islands to keep riders guessing.

ENDER DRAGON HEAD

For the grand finale, take your roller coaster right through the jaws of a giant ender dragon head. This one is lit up with End rods.

OBSIDIAN PILLARS
Create small versions of the main island's obsidian pillars and add End crystals on top.

END TERRAIN
I built several islands out of End stone, then constructed End stone brick paths between them and placed rails on top.

OUTER ISLAND FEATURES
Add some chorus plants to each island, then choose a spot to build an Outer Island tower and an End ship. Take your ride through the tower and the ship. See page 56 for a ship tutorial.

END FEATURES

Now let's move on to the End features for your Alternate Dimensions Ride. These tips will help you build a convincing End ship and a truly terrifying dragon head to finish off the ride in a suitably dramatic fashion.

END SHIP

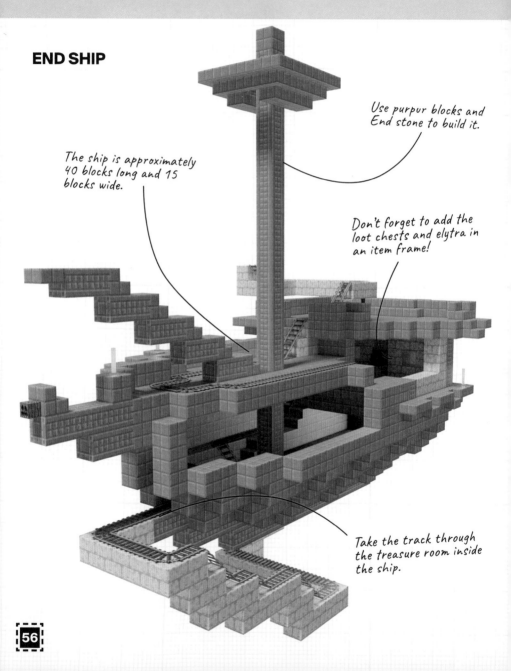

Use purpur blocks and End stone to build it.

The ship is approximately 40 blocks long and 15 blocks wide.

Don't forget to add the loot chests and elytra in an item frame!

Take the track through the treasure room inside the ship.

ENDER DRAGON HEAD

The head should be around 12 blocks wide and 12 blocks high.

Use black concrete for the face and gray concrete for the ears.

Magenta and pink concrete work well for the eyes.

Take the track through the mouth and out the back of the dragon head.

Make sure the mouth is open wide enough for the track to run through it.

DECORATIVE EXTRAS

Your theme park is almost ready to open to the public! This is so exciting! But before you open your doors to your eager friends, there are just a few small details left to add. Let's take a look at some decorative extras.

ENTRANCE

Build a low wall around your theme park, then create a wide entrance where your friends can access the park. Use lots of brightly colored concrete blocks and don't forget to add plenty of light sources (torches, redstone torches, glowstone etc).

FERRIS WHEEL MAP STAND

Although ferris wheels don't actually spin in Minecraft, no theme park is complete without one. So, what better way to welcome your friends into your park than by having them visit a model of a ferris wheel to grab a handy map? Place several chests underneath the ferris wheel with a sign saying "MAPS," and don't forget to tell your visitors to pick one up!

CREATING AND CLONING A MAP

Find a blank map in your Creative mode inventory, then add it to one of your hotbar slots and hit the "use item" button. Walk around your park until it has mapped the area. Combine this map with a blank map on an anvil, and you will end up with two maps of your park. Keep combining maps on your anvil like this until you have enough for all your visitors.

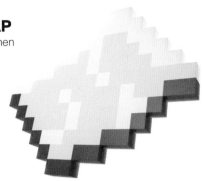

SNACK STANDS

Build a few decorative snack stands around your park. No matter what mode you're playing in, they help make your theme park look authentic. If you're playing in Survival mode, you can fill chests with food so players can grab something to eat to top up their hunger.

BEACH AREA

Create a small area of sandy beach and give your guests a nice place to relax in when they've finished riding on the water slides. Build sun loungers from quartz stairs and slabs, and parasols from colored blocks and fences.

AERIAL WALKWAY

Wow – with all those extra details added in, your park is looking truly amazing! There's one finishing touch you can add, which will allow everyone to view the whole park from up high and marvel at your building skills. Let's finish off with an aerial walkway!

Build your aerial walkway around the outer perimeter of your park – 20-30 blocks above the ground is a good height.

Place pillars underneath the walkway, with ladders attached to the sides – these are the access points where players can climb up and down from the walkway.

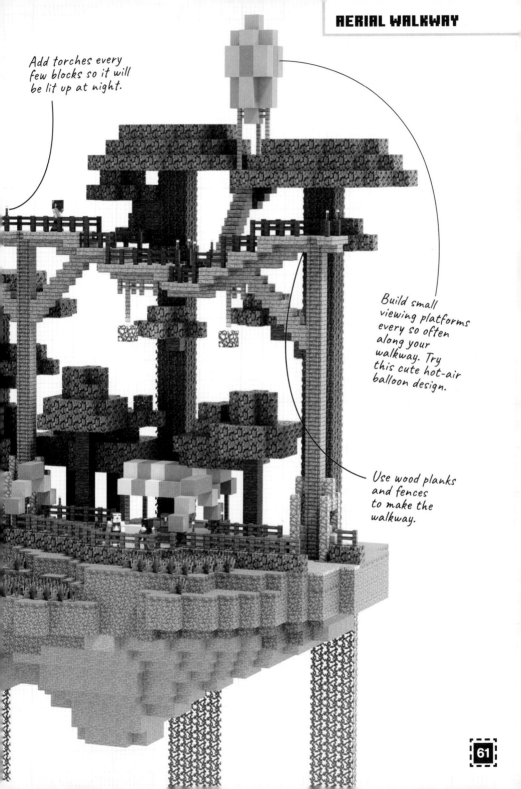

Add torches every few blocks so it will be lit up at night.

Build small viewing platforms every so often along your walkway. Try this cute hot-air balloon design.

Use wood planks and fences to make the walkway.

61

BYE FOR NOW!

Gosh, that was fun! I hope my building ideas and tips helped you to build an epic theme park of your own, and I'm sure you and your friends will enjoy your rides for a long time to come. Don't be afraid to experiment with your own designs, too!

Ooh, I've just had another idea for an epic build project, so maybe I'll have something else to share with you soon!

Keep building!

Sparks

STAY IN THE KNOW!

Learn about the latest Minecraft books when you sign up for our newsletter at **ReadMinecraft.com**

DEL REY

MOJANG